Ella Dawn Creations

Soon To Be Mr. & Mrs.

_____

Wedding Date:

_____

Wedding Planner

WEDDING DATE & TIME:

TO DO LIST:

VENUE ADDRESS:

BUDGET:

OFFICIANT:

WEDDING PARTY:

NOTES & REMINDERS:

Wedding Budget Planner

	BUDGET:	TOTAL COST:	TOTAL PAID:
WEDDING VENUE			
RECEPTION VENUE			
FLORIST			
OFFICIANT			
CATERER			
WEDDING CAKE			
BRIDAL ATTIRE			
GROOM ATTIRE			
BRIDAL JEWELRY			
BRIDESMAID ATTIRE			
GROOMSMEN ATTIRE			
HAIR & MAKE UP			
PHOTOGRAPHER			
VIDEOGRAPHER			
DJ SERVICE/ENTERTAINMENT			
INVITATIONS			
TRANSPORTATION			
WEDDING PARTY GIFTS			
RENTALS			
HONEYMOON			

12 Months Before

SET THE DATE	CONSIDER FLORISTS
SET YOUR BUDGET	RESEARCH CATERERS
CHOOSE A DESTINATION	DECIDE ON OFFICIANT
REQUEST PHOTOS FROM RESORT	CREATE INITIAL GUEST LIST
RESEARCH VENUES	CHOOSE WEDDING PARTY
BOOK A WEDDING PLANNER	SHOP FOR WEDDING DRESS
RESEARCH PHOTOGRAPHERS	REGISTER WITH GIFT REGISTRY
RESEARCH VIDEOGRAPHERS	DISCUSS HONEYMOON IDEAS
RESEARCH DJ'S/ENTERTAINMENT	RESEARCH WEDDING RINGS

THINGS TO REMEMBER:

9 Months Before

FINALIZE GUEST LIST	CHOOSE WEDDING GOWN
ORDER INVITATIONS	ORDER BRIDESMAIDS DRESSES
PLAN YOUR RECEPTION	RESERVE TUXEDOS
BOOK PHOTOGRAPHER	ARRANGE TRANSPORTATION
BOOK VIDEOGRAPHER	BOOK WEDDING VENUE
BOOK FLORIST	BOOK RECEPTION VENUE
BOOK DJ/ENTERTAINMENT	PLAN HONEYMOON
BOOK CATERER	BOOK OFFICIANT
CHOOSE WEDDING CAKE	BOOK ROOMS FOR GUESTS

THINGS TO REMEMBER:

6 Months Before

ORDER THANK YOU NOTES

REVIEW RECEPTION DETAILS

MAKE APPT FOR DRESS FITTING

CONFIRM BRIDEMAIDS DRESSES

BOOK BLOCK OF HOTEL ROOMS
(FOR GUESTS)

BOOK HAIR/MAKE UP STYLIST

CONFIRM MUSIC SELECTIONS

PLAN BRIDAL SHOWER

CREATE YOUR GIFT REGISTERY

SHOP FOR WEDDING RINGS

THINGS TO REMEMBER:

3 Months Before

MAIL OUT INVITATIONS	FINALIZE RECEPTION MENU
MEET WITH OFFICIANT	PLAN REHEARSAL DINNER
BUY GIFTS FOR WEDDING PARTY	CONFIRM ALL BOOKINGS
BOOK FINAL GOWN FITTING	APPLY FOR MARRIAGE LICENSE
GET VACCINES OR BLOOD TESTS (IF NEEDED)	CONFIRM MUSIC SELECTIONS
PLAN YOUR HAIR STYLE	DRAFT WEDDING VOWS
SHOP FOR RESORT/HONEYMOON	BOOK FLIGHT & ACCOMMODATIONS
CONFIRM PASSPORTS ARE VALID	ARRANGE AIRPORT TRANSFER

THINGS TO REMEMBER:

1 Month Before

CONFIRM FINAL GUEST COUNT	REHEARSE WEDDING VOWS
CONFIRM RECEPTION DETAILS	BOOK MANI-PEDI
ATTEND FINAL GOWN FITTING	CONFIRM WITH FLORIST
CONFIRM PHOTOGRAPHER	CONFIRM VIDEOGRAPHER
WRAP WEDDING PARTY GIFTS	PICK UP BRIDEMAIDS DRESSES
CREATE PHOTOGRAPHY SHOT LIST	CREATE WEDDING SCHEDULE

THINGS TO REMEMBER:

1 Week Before

FINALIZE SEATING PLANS

MAKE PAYMENTS TO VENDORS

PACK FOR HONEYMOON

CONFIRM HOTEL RESERVATIONS

GIVE SCHEDULE TO PARTY

DELIVER LICENSE TO OFFICIANT

CONFIRM WITH BAKERY

PICK UP WEDDING DRESS

PICK UP TUXEDOS

GIVE MUSIC LIST TO DJ

THINGS TO REMEMBER:

1 Day Before

GET MANICURE/PEDICURE

ATTEND REHEARSAL DINNER

GET A GOOD NIGHT'S SLEEP!

GIVE GIFTS TO WEDDING PARTY

FINALIZE PACKING

TO DO LIST:

The Big Day!

GET HAIR & MAKE UP DONE   MEET WITH BRIDESMAIDS

HAVE A HEALTHY BREAKFAST   GIVE RINGS TO BEST MAN

ENJOY YOUR BIG DAY!

TO DO LIST:

Wedding Events

ENGAGEMENT PARTY:

DATE: LOCATION:

TIME: NUMBER OF GUESTS:

  NOTES:

BRIDAL SHOWER:

DATE: LOCATION:

TIME: NUMBER OF GUESTS:

  NOTES:

BACHELORETTE PARTY:

DATE: LOCATION:

TIME: NUMBER OF GUESTS:

  NOTES:

Wedding Events

BACHELOR PARTY:

DATE: LOCATION:

TIME: NUMBER OF GUESTS:

NOTES:

REHEARSAL DINNER:

DATE: LOCATION:

TIME: NUMBER OF GUESTS:

NOTES:

DAY-AFTER BRUNCH:

DATE: LOCATION:

TIME: NUMBER OF GUESTS:

NOTES:

Wedding Events

CEREMONY REHEARSAL:

DATE: LOCATION:

TIME: NUMBER OF GUESTS:

NOTES:

PHOTOGRAPHY SHOOT:

DATE: LOCATION:

TIME: NUMBER OF GUESTS:

NOTES:

RECEPTION:

DATE: LOCATION:

TIME: NUMBER OF GUESTS:

NOTES:

Wedding Party (the Girls)

MAID/MATRON OF HONOR:

PHONE: DRESS SIZE: SHOE SIZE:

EMAIL:

BRIDESMAID #1:

PHONE: DRESS SIZE: SHOE SIZE:

EMAIL:

BRIDESMAID #2:

PHONE: DRESS SIZE: SHOE SIZE:

EMAIL:

BRIDESMAID #3:

PHONE: DRESS SIZE: SHOE SIZE:

EMAIL:

BRIDESMAID #4:

PHONE: DRESS SIZE: SHOE SIZE:

EMAIL:

NOTES:

Wedding Party (the Girls)

NOTES:

BRIDESMAID #5:

PHONE: DRESS SIZE: SHOE SIZE:

EMAIL:

BRIDESMAID #6:

PHONE: DRESS SIZE: SHOE SIZE:

EMAIL:

BRIDESMAID #7:

PHONE: DRESS SIZE: SHOE SIZE:

EMAIL:

BRIDESMAID #8:

PHONE: DRESS SIZE: SHOE SIZE:

EMAIL:

Wedding Party (the Guys)

BEST MAN:

PHONE: WAIST SIZE: SHOE SIZE:

NECK SIZE: SLEEVE SIZE: JACKET SIZE:

EMAIL:

GROOMSMEN #1:

PHONE: WAIST SIZE: SHOE SIZE:

NECK SIZE: SLEEVE SIZE: JACKET SIZE:

EMAIL:

GROOMSMEN #2:

PHONE: WAIST SIZE: SHOE SIZE:

NECK SIZE: SLEEVE SIZE: JACKET SIZE:

EMAIL:

GROOMSMEN #3:

PHONE: WAIST SIZE: SHOE SIZE:

NECK SIZE: SLEEVE SIZE: JACKET SIZE:

EMAIL:

GROOMSMEN #4:

PHONE: WAIST SIZE: SHOE SIZE:

NECK SIZE: SLEEVE SIZE: JACKET SIZE:

EMAIL:

Wedding Party (the Guys)

NOTES:

GROOMSMEN #5:

PHONE: WAIST SIZE: SHOE SIZE:

NECK SIZE: SLEEVE SIZE: JACKET SIZE:

EMAIL:

GROOMSMEN #6:

PHONE: WAIST SIZE: SHOE SIZE:

NECK SIZE: SLEEVE SIZE: JACKET SIZE:

EMAIL:

GROOMSMEN #7:

PHONE: WAIST SIZE: SHOE SIZE:

NECK SIZE: SLEEVE SIZE: JACKET SIZE:

EMAIL:

GROOMSMEN #8:

PHONE: WAIST SIZE: SHOE SIZE:

NECK SIZE: SLEEVE SIZE: JACKET SIZE:

EMAIL:

Photographer

PHOTOGRAPHER:

PHONE: COMPANY:

EMAIL: ADDRESS:

WEDDING PACKAGE OVERVIEW:

EST PRICE:

INCLUSIONS:	YES ✓	NO ✓	COST:
ENGAGEMENT SHOOT:			
PHOTO ALBUMS:			
FRAMES:			
PROOFS INCLUDED:			
NEGATIVES INCLUDED:			
TOTAL COST:			

Videographer

VIDEOGRAPHER:

PHONE: COMPANY:

EMAIL: ADDRESS:

WEDDING PACKAGE OVERVIEW:

EST PRICE:

INCLUSIONS: YES ✓   NO ✓   COST:

DUPLICATES/COPIES:

PHOTO MONTAGE:

MUSIC ADDED:

EDITING:

TOTAL COST:

NOTES:

DJ/Entertainment

DJ/LIVE BAND/ENTERTAINMENT:

PHONE: _____ COMPANY: _____

EMAIL: _____ ADDRESS: _____

START TIME: _____ END TIME: _____

ENTERTAINMENT SERVICE OVERVIEW:

EST PRICE: _____

INCLUSIONS:	YES ✓	NO ✓	COST:
SOUND EQUIPMENT:			
LIGHTING:			
SPECIAL EFFECTS:			
GRATUITIES			

TOTAL COST: _____

NOTES:

Florist

FLORIST:

PHONE: COMPANY:

EMAIL: ADDRESS:

FLORAL PACKAGE:

EST PRICE: ....

INCLUSIONS: YES ✓   NO ✓   COST:

BRIDAL BOUQUET:

THROW AWAY BOUQUET:

CORSAGES:

CEREMONY FLOWERS

CENTERPIECES

CAKE TOPPER

BOUTONNIERE

TOTAL COST:

Wedding Cake/Baker

PHONE: _____ COMPANY: _____

EMAIL: _____ ADDRESS: _____

WEDDING CAKE PACKAGE:

COST: _____ FREE TASTING: _____ DELIVERY FEE: _____

FLAVOR:

FILLING:

SIZE:

SHAPE:

COLOR:

EXTRAS:

TOTAL COST:

NOTES:

Transportation Planner

TO CEREMONY: PICK UP TIME: PICK UP LOCATION:

BRIDE:

GROOM:

BRIDE'S PARENTS:

GROOM'S PARENTS:

BRIDESMAIDS:

GROOMSMEN:

NOTES:

TO RECEPTION: PICK UP TIME: PICK UP LOCATION:

BRIDE & GROOM:

BRIDE'S PARENTS:

GROOM'S PARENTS:

BRIDESMAIDS:

GROOMSMEN:

Names & Addresses

CEREMONY:

PHONE: CONTACT NAME:

EMAIL: ADDRESS:

RECEPTION:

PHONE: CONTACT NAME:

EMAIL: ADDRESS:

OFFICIANT:

PHONE: CONTACT NAME:

EMAIL: ADDRESS:

WEDDING PLANNER:

PHONE: CONTACT NAME:

EMAIL: ADDRESS:

CATERER:

PHONE: CONTACT NAME:

EMAIL: ADDRESS:

FLORIST:

PHONE: CONTACT NAME:

EMAIL: ADDRESS:

Names & Addresses

BAKERY:

PHONE:

CONTACT NAME:

EMAIL:

ADDRESS:

BRIDAL SHOP:

PHONE:

CONTACT NAME:

EMAIL:

ADDRESS:

PHOTOGRAPHER:

PHONE:

CONTACT NAME:

EMAIL:

ADDRESS:

VIDEOGRAPHER:

PHONE:

CONTACT NAME:

EMAIL:

ADDRESS:

DJ/ENTERTAINMENT:

PHONE:

CONTACT NAME:

EMAIL:

ADDRESS:

HAIR/NAIL SALON:

PHONE:

CONTACT NAME:

EMAIL:

ADDRESS:

Names & Addresses

MAKE UP ARTIST:

PHONE: CONTACT NAME:

EMAIL: ADDRESS:

RENTALS:

PHONE: CONTACT NAME:

EMAIL: ADDRESS:

HONEYMOON RESORT/HOTEL:

PHONE: CONTACT NAME:

EMAIL: ADDRESS:

TRANSPORTATION SERVICE:

PHONE: CONTACT NAME:

EMAIL: ADDRESS:

NOTES:

Caterer Details

CONTACT INFORMATION:

PHONE: CONTACT NAME:

EMAIL: ADDRESS:

MENU CHOICE #1:

MENU CHOICE #2:

	YES ✓	NO ✓	COST:
BAR INCLUDED:			
CORKAGE FEE:			
HORS D'OEUVRES:			
TAXES INCLUDED:			
GRATUITIES INCLUDED:			

Menu Planner

HORS D'OEUVRES

1st COURSE:

2nd COURSE:

3rd COURSE:

4th COURSE:

DESSERT:

1 Week Before

	THINGS TO DO:	NOTES:
MONDAY		
TUESDAY		
WEDNESDAY		
THURSDAY		

REMINDERS & NOTES:

1 Week Before

	THINGS TO DO:	NOTES:
FRIDAY		
SATURDAY		
SUNDAY		

LEFT TO DO:

REMINDERS: NOTES:

Wedding Guest List

NAME:	ADDRESS:	# IN PARTY:	RSVP: ✓

Wedding Guest List

NAME:	ADDRESS:	# IN PARTY:	RSVP: ✓

Wedding Guest List

NAME:	ADDRESS:	# IN PARTY:	RSVP: ✓

Wedding Guest List

NAME:	ADDRESS:	# IN PARTY:	RSVP: ✓

Wedding Guest List

NAME:	ADDRESS:	# IN PARTY:	RSVP: ✓

Wedding Guest List

NAME:	ADDRESS:	# IN PARTY:	RSVP: ✓

Wedding Guest List

NAME:	ADDRESS:	# IN PARTY:	RSVP: ✓

Wedding Guest List

NAME:	ADDRESS:	# IN PARTY:	RSVP: ✓

Wedding Guest List

NAME:	ADDRESS:	# IN PARTY:	RSVP: ✓

Wedding Guest List

NAME:	ADDRESS:	# IN PARTY:	RSVP: ✓

Wedding Guest List

NAME:	ADDRESS:	# IN PARTY:	RSVP: ✓

Wedding Guest List

NAME:	ADDRESS:	# IN PARTY:	RSVP: ✓

Wedding Guest List

NAME:	ADDRESS:	# IN PARTY:	RSVP: ✓

Wedding Guest List

NAME:	ADDRESS:	# IN PARTY:	RSVP: ✓

Wedding Guest List

NAME:	ADDRESS:	# IN PARTY:	RSVP: ✓

Wedding Guest List

NAME:	ADDRESS:	# IN PARTY:	RSVP: ✓

Wedding Guest List

NAME:	ADDRESS:	# IN PARTY:	RSVP: ✓

Wedding Guest List

NAME:	ADDRESS:	# IN PARTY:	RSVP: ✓

Wedding Guest List

NAME:	ADDRESS:	# IN PARTY:	RSVP: ✓

Wedding Guest List

NAME:	ADDRESS:	# IN PARTY:	RSVP: ✓

Wedding Guest List

NAME:	ADDRESS:	# IN PARTY:	RSVP: ✓

Wedding Guest List

NAME:	ADDRESS:	# IN PARTY:	RSVP: ✓

Wedding Guest List

NAME:	ADDRESS:	# IN PARTY:	RSVP: ✓

Wedding Guest List

NAME:	ADDRESS:	# IN PARTY:	RSVP: ✓

Wedding Guest List

NAME:	ADDRESS:	# IN PARTY:	RSVP: ✓

Wedding Guest List

NAME:	ADDRESS:	# IN PARTY:	RSVP: ✓

Wedding Guest List

NAME:	ADDRESS:	# IN PARTY:	RSVP: ✓

Wedding Guest List

NAME:	ADDRESS:	# IN PARTY:	RSVP: ✓

Wedding Guest List

NAME:	ADDRESS:	# IN PARTY:	RSVP: ✓

Wedding Guest List

NAME:	ADDRESS:	# IN PARTY:	RSVP: ✓

Wedding Guest List

NAME:	ADDRESS:	# IN PARTY:	RSVP: ✓

Wedding Guest List

NAME:	ADDRESS:	# IN PARTY:	RSVP: ✓

Wedding Guest List

NAME:	ADDRESS:	# IN PARTY:	RSVP: ✓

Seating Chart Planner

Table #

Table #

Table #

Table #

SEATING PLANNER NOTES:

Seating Chart Planner

Table #

Table #

Table #

Table #

SEATING PLANNER NOTES:

Seating Chart Planner

Table #

Table #

Table #

Table #

SEATING PLANNER NOTES:

Seating Chart Planner

Table #

Table #

Table #

Table #

SEATING PLANNER NOTES:

Seating Chart Planner

Table #

Table #

Table #

Table #

SEATING PLANNER NOTES:

Seating Chart Planner

Table #

Table #

Table #

Table #

SEATING PLANNER NOTES:

Seating Chart Planner

Table #

Table #

Table #

Table #

SEATING PLANNER NOTES:

Seating Chart Planner

Table #

Table #

Table #

Table #

SEATING PLANNER NOTES:

Seating Chart Planner

Table #

Table #

Table #

Table #

SEATING PLANNER NOTES:

Seating Chart Planner

Table #

Table #

Table #

Table #

SEATING PLANNER NOTES:

Seating Chart Planner

Table #

Table #

Table #

Table #

SEATING PLANNER NOTES:

Seating Chart Planner

Table #

Table #

Table #

Table #

SEATING PLANNER NOTES:

Seating Chart Planner

Table #

Table #

Table #

Table #

SEATING PLANNER NOTES:

Seating Chart Planner

Table #

Table #

Table #

Table #

SEATING PLANNER NOTES:

Seating Chart Planner

Table #

Table #

Table #

Table #

SEATING PLANNER NOTES:

Seating Chart Planner

Table #

Table #

Table #

Table #

SEATING PLANNER NOTES:

Seating Chart Planner

Table #

Table #

Table #

Table #

SEATING PLANNER NOTES:

Seating Chart Planner

Table #

Table #

Table #

Table #

SEATING PLANNER NOTES:

Seating Chart Planner

Table #

Table #

Table #

Table #

SEATING PLANNER NOTES:

Wedding Checklist

THINGS TO REMEMBER: DATE:

NOTES:

Wedding Checklist

THINGS TO REMEMBER: DATE: ✓

NOTES:

Wedding Checklist

THINGS TO REMEMBER: DATE:

NOTES:

Wedding Checklist

THINGS TO REMEMBER: **DATE:**

✓

NOTES:

Wedding Checklist

THINGS TO REMEMBER: DATE:

NOTES:

Wedding Checklist

THINGS TO REMEMBER:　　　　　　**DATE:**

✓

NOTES:

Wedding Checklist

THINGS TO REMEMBER: DATE:

NOTES:

Wedding Checklist

THINGS TO REMEMBER: DATE:

NOTES:

Wedding Checklist

THINGS TO REMEMBER: DATE:

NOTES:

Wedding Checklist

THINGS TO REMEMBER: **DATE:**   ✓

NOTES:

Wedding Checklist

THINGS TO REMEMBER: DATE:

NOTES:

Wedding Checklist

THINGS TO REMEMBER: **DATE:**

☑
☐
☐
☐
☐
☐
☐
☐
☐
☐
☐

NOTES:

Wedding Checklist

THINGS TO REMEMBER: **DATE:**

NOTES:

Wedding Checklist

THINGS TO REMEMBER: DATE: ✓

☐
☐
☐
☐
☐
☐
☐
☐
☐
☐
☐
☐

NOTES:

Wedding Checklist

THINGS TO REMEMBER: DATE:

NOTES:

Wedding Checklist

THINGS TO REMEMBER: DATE: ✓

NOTES:

Wedding Checklist

THINGS TO REMEMBER: DATE:

NOTES:

Wedding Checklist

THINGS TO REMEMBER: **DATE:**   ✓

NOTES:

Wedding Checklist

THINGS TO REMEMBER: DATE:

NOTES:

Wedding Checklist

THINGS TO REMEMBER: **DATE:**   ✓

☐
☐
☐
☐
☐
☐
☐
☐
☐
☐
☐
☐

NOTES:

Wedding Checklist

THINGS TO REMEMBER: DATE:

NOTES:

Wedding Checklist

THINGS TO REMEMBER: **DATE:**

✓

NOTES:

Wedding Checklist

THINGS TO REMEMBER: DATE:

NOTES:

Wedding Checklist

THINGS TO REMEMBER: **DATE:**   ✓

NOTES:

Wedding Checklist

THINGS TO REMEMBER: DATE:

NOTES:

Wedding Checklist

THINGS TO REMEMBER: **DATE:**   ✓

NOTES:

Wedding Checklist

THINGS TO REMEMBER: DATE:

NOTES:

Wedding Checklist

THINGS TO REMEMBER: **DATE:**

✓

☐
☐
☐
☐
☐
☐
☐
☐
☐
☐
☐

NOTES:

Wedding Checklist

THINGS TO REMEMBER: DATE:

NOTES:

Wedding Checklist

THINGS TO REMEMBER: **DATE:**

✓

NOTES:

Wedding Checklist

THINGS TO REMEMBER: DATE:

NOTES:

Wedding Checklist

THINGS TO REMEMBER: **DATE:**   ✓

NOTES:

Wedding Checklist

THINGS TO REMEMBER: DATE:

NOTES:

Wedding Checklist

THINGS TO REMEMBER: **DATE:**

NOTES:

Wedding Checklist

THINGS TO REMEMBER: **DATE:**

NOTES:

Wedding Checklist

THINGS TO REMEMBER: **DATE:**

✓

☐
☐
☐
☐
☐
☐
☐
☐
☐
☐
☐
☐

NOTES:

Made in the USA
Las Vegas, NV
13 February 2022

43841069R00073